NATHAN MacKINNON
HOCKEY SUPERSTAR

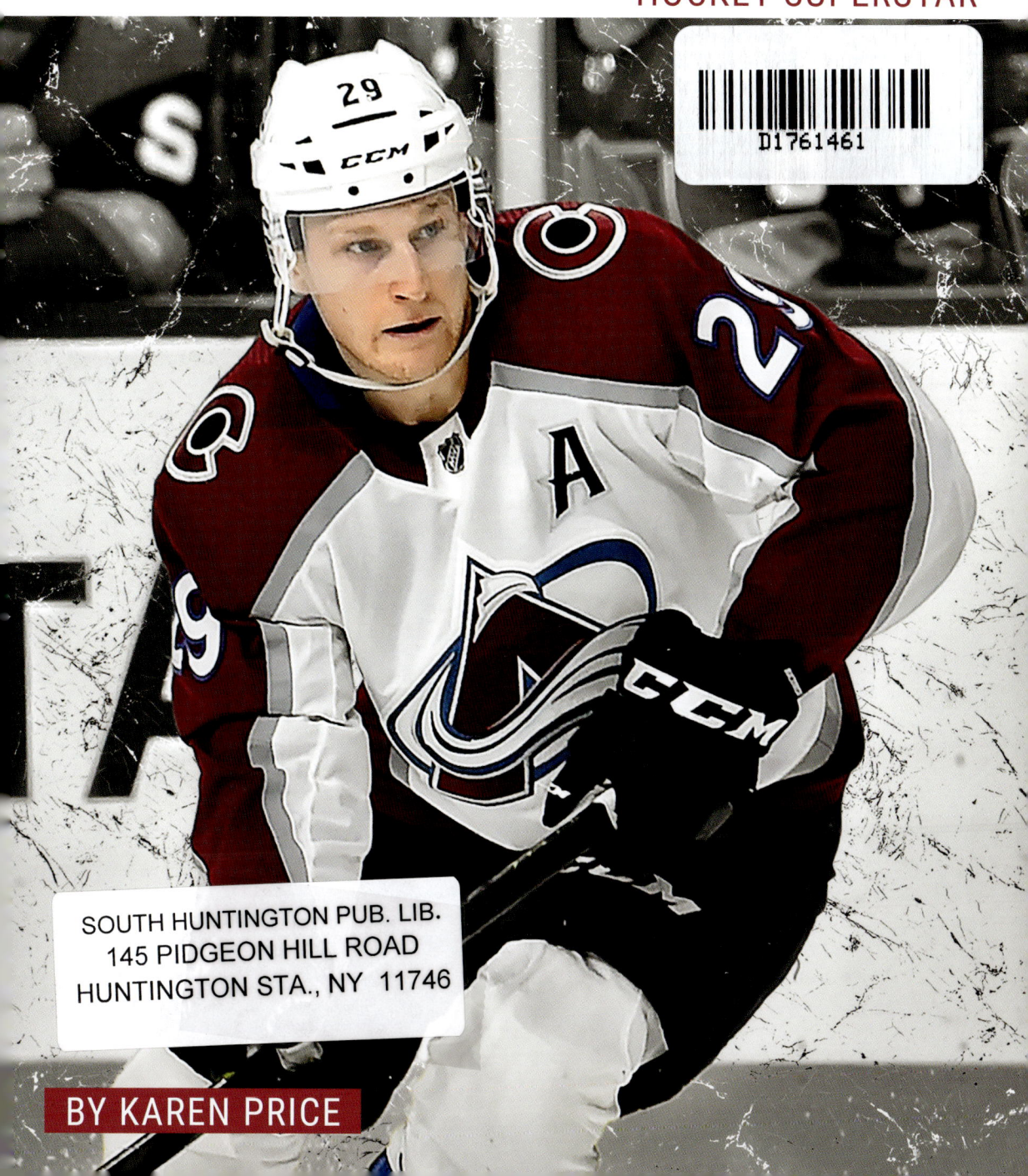

BY KAREN PRICE

Copyright © 2020 by Press Room Editions. All rights reserved. No part of this book may be used or reproduced in any manner whatsoever, including internet usage, without written permission from the copyright owner, except in the case of brief quotations embodied in critical articles and reviews.

First Edition
First Printing, 2019

Book design by Jake Nordby
Cover design by Jake Nordby
Photographs ©: David Becker/AP Images, cover, 1; Matthew Stockman/Getty Images Sport/Getty Images, 4; Jack Dempsey/AP Images, 7, 8; marinat197/Shutterstock Images, 8–9; Liam Richards/The Canadian Press/AP Images, 10, 13; Bill Kostroun/AP Images, 15; David Zalubowski/AP Images, 16–17; Steven King/Icon Sportswire, 19; Dustin Bradford/Icon Sportswire, 21; Jeanine Leech/Icon Sportswire, 22, 30; Jim Mone/AP Images, 24; Brett Holmes/Icon Sportswire, 27; Red Line Editorial, 29

Press Box Books, an imprint of Press Room Editions.

Library of Congress Control Number: 2019936729

ISBN
978-1-63494-101-3 (library bound)
978-1-63494-110-5 (paperback)
978-1-63494-119-8 (epub)
978-1-63494-128-0 (hosted ebook)

Distributed by North Star Editions, Inc.
2297 Waters Drive
Mendota Heights, MN 55120
www.northstareditions.com

Printed in the United States of America

About the Author
Karen Price grew up outside Philadelphia, graduated from the University of Colorado, and has called Pittsburgh home since 2002. She has been writing about sports for more than 20 years and has covered both the Colorado Avalanche and Pittsburgh Penguins.

TABLE OF CONTENTS

CHAPTER 1
Playoff Bound 5

CHAPTER 2
Junior League Star 11

CHAPTER 3
Rookie Sensation 17

CHAPTER 4
Becoming a Superstar 23

Timeline • 28
At-a-Glance • 30
Glossary • 31
To Learn More • 32
Index • 32

1 PLAYOFF BOUND

Nathan MacKinnon wasn't ready to go home. He and the Colorado Avalanche were playing the St. Louis Blues in the final game of the 2017-18 regular season. The team that won would clinch the final spot in the Stanley Cup playoffs. And for the team that lost, the season would be over.

The Avs scored the game's first two goals. But the Blues pulled within one midway through the second period. That was too close for MacKinnon. With just

MacKinnon takes the puck behind the net during a 2018 game against the St. Louis Blues.

over three minutes left in the period, Avalanche captain Gabriel Landeskog had the puck along the left boards. He circled back, looking for a play. Then he dished the puck to MacKinnon, who was skating past him.

MacKinnon took a few strides and snapped the puck toward the net. The clink of the puck hitting metal echoed through the arena. MacKinnon's shot had found the top corner. The goal horn blared, and the Colorado fans leaped to their feet. The Avs were up 3–1.

MacKinnon's goal turned out to be the game-winner.

SPEED SKATER

Nathan MacKinnon is known for his speed. In 2014 he took part in a race against Canadian speed skater Charles Hamelin, winner of three Olympic gold medals. The race was from blue line to blue line. MacKinnon was decked out in full hockey gear, while Hamelin wore a sleek racing suit. Even so, MacKinnon won the race by a stride.

Colorado fans erupt in cheers after MacKinnon scores a goal.

One of the best players in the National Hockey League (NHL) had just helped his team reach the playoffs for the first time in four years.

HAT TRICK!

Nathan MacKinnon scored his first career hat trick on February 22, 2015. Each goal used a different type of shot.

1. In the first period, MacKinnon received a pass near his own blue line. He sped all the way down the ice, beating two defenders. Then he snapped a backhand shot past the goalie's glove side.

2. Early in the second period, Avs forward Ryan O'Reilly launched a slap shot. MacKinnon deflected it into the net for a goal.

3. Later in the second period, MacKinnon streaked down the ice on a breakaway. He blasted a wrist shot into the back of the net.

2 JUNIOR LEAGUE STAR

Nathan MacKinnon was born on September 1, 1995. He grew up in Cole Harbour, Nova Scotia, just outside Halifax. From a young age, it was clear that Nathan had some serious hockey skills. People started comparing him to Sidney Crosby. The Pittsburgh Penguins star had grown up in the same town.

As a teenager, Nathan moved to Minnesota to attend Shattuck-St. Mary's. The private school is well known for producing some of the best hockey

Nathan MacKinnon lets out a scream after scoring a goal for the Halifax Mooseheads in 2013.

FAMOUS FRIEND

During the offseason, Nathan MacKinnon and Sidney Crosby are neighbors. The pair has also appeared together in commercials for a Canadian restaurant chain. In one ad, they served customers at a drive-through. In another ad, they surprised a hockey team from Kenya and played alongside them.

players in North America. In fact, Crosby had also gone to school there. By the time Nathan left the school, he was well prepared for his junior hockey career.

In the 2011 Quebec Major Junior Hockey League draft, Nathan was selected first overall by the Baie-Comeau Drakkar. There was just one problem. Nathan didn't want to play for the Drakkar. So, they traded him to the Halifax Mooseheads.

Nathan didn't waste any time showing how good he was. During one game, he scored an incredible five goals. Nathan finished the season with 78 points in 58 games. He also

Nathan attempts to skate past a defender during a 2013 game against the London Knights.

finished second in the league's rookie of the year voting.

Nathan missed parts of the next season with a knee injury, but the best was yet to come. In 2013, Halifax beat Baie-Comeau to win the league championship. With that victory, the Mooseheads were headed to the Canadian Hockey League championship. This tournament determines the best team in Canada's three junior leagues.

Going into the third period of the final game, Halifax was clinging to a one-goal lead against the Portland Winterhawks. That's when Nathan scored his second goal of the game, helping the Mooseheads win their first Memorial Cup.

By that time, Nathan was already one of the top prospects in the upcoming NHL Entry Draft. Scouts liked his burst of speed, his hockey sense, and his instincts. He could accelerate much faster than most players, plus he was smart and knew how to finish. He always seemed to know just where he needed to be. And with his stickhandling skills, he could make passes that most other players couldn't.

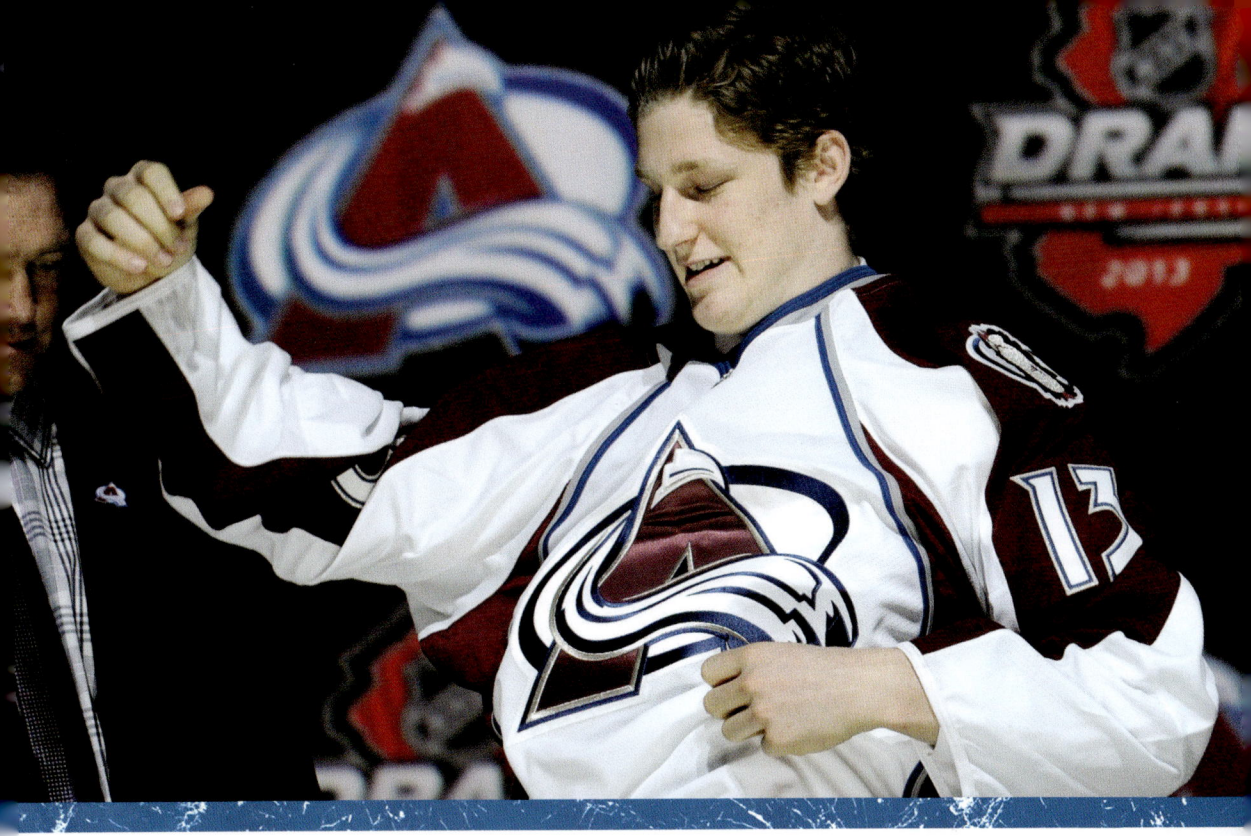

Nathan tries on his new Avalanche jersey after being selected No. 1 overall in 2013.

The Colorado Avalanche had the first pick in the draft. General manager Joe Sakic stepped to the microphone to make the announcement. The Avalanche selected Nathan MacKinnon with the No. 1 overall pick. Now Nathan had something else in common with Sidney Crosby. Crosby had been the top pick in 2005.

3 ROOKIE SENSATION

Nathan MacKinnon made his debut with the Avalanche in October 2013. He had turned 18 just a month earlier. That made him the youngest player ever to suit up for the Avalanche. MacKinnon had two assists in his first game, and the Avalanche beat the Anaheim Ducks 6–1.

A few months later, he put together a record-breaking point streak. It started in January 2014 with an assist against the Tampa Bay Lightning. In the next game, he scored a goal. And in the game

MacKinnon surges down the ice during his first NHL game.

17

after that, he had a goal and an assist. After five weeks, MacKinnon's point streak was still going strong.

In early March, the Avalanche were in Detroit to play the Red Wings. In the last minute of overtime, MacKinnon skated the puck into the offensive zone. His shot went wide, and he circled behind the net to pick up the loose puck. That's when he saw Avs defenseman Andre Benoit sneaking down the opposite side. MacKinnon threaded a pass to his teammate, and Benoit scored.

HOUSE GUEST

Young NHL players often move in with veteran teammates. Nathan MacKinnon spent his rookie season living with goalie Jean-Sebastien Giguere and his family. MacKinnon felt grateful having an older player who was willing to teach him about the game. Giguere joked that MacKinnon was a bit messy, but he was glad to have the young star in his house. So were Giguere's three young sons. They often played video games with MacKinnon.

MacKinnon makes the pass that will break a record held by Wayne Gretzky.

With that assist, MacKinnon broke one of Wayne Gretzky's records. MacKinnon's 13-game point streak was the longest ever by an 18-year-old in the NHL.

MacKinnon was having a great season, and so were the Avalanche. After coming in last the previous season, they finished first in their division. MacKinnon was about to get his first taste of the NHL playoffs.

Colorado faced the Minnesota Wild in the first round. In the opening game of the series, MacKinnon assisted on the game-tying goal with seconds left in regulation. Then in overtime, he assisted on the game-winner.

In Game 2, the Avalanche trailed 1–0 in the first period. Then MacKinnon took charge as he carried the puck into the offensive zone. Two defenders were in front of him, and another was chasing from behind. But MacKinnon somehow slipped through the traffic and blew a shot past the goalie. It was his first NHL playoff goal. He had three more assists in the game, helping the Avs build a 2–0 lead in the series.

Even though Colorado lost the series in Game 7, MacKinnon still had something big on

MacKinnon makes a move during a 2014 playoff game against the Minnesota Wild.

the horizon. In June 2014, he won the Calder Memorial Trophy as the NHL rookie of the year. The vote was almost unanimous. And MacKinnon was the youngest Calder Trophy winner ever.

4 BECOMING A SUPERSTAR

There's no way around it. The next three seasons were rough for the Avalanche. Nathan MacKinnon recorded his first hat trick in 2015, but he didn't match the point total from his rookie year. Things got even worse during the 2016–17 season. The Avalanche won only 22 games and finished last in the league. But that was about to change.

In November 2017, MacKinnon racked up 5 goals and 15 assists in just 12 games. His best night came against

MacKinnon leads an attack during a 2015 game against the Pittsburgh Penguins.

MacKinnon puts the puck in the net against the Minnesota Wild in 2018.

the Washington Capitals. In the first period, MacKinnon skated into position and received a pass from defenseman Samuel Girard. Then he weaved through traffic and scored on the glove side. MacKinnon also collected four assists that night as Colorado crushed Washington 6–2. It was the first five-point game of his career.

MacKinnon wasn't done yet. Later in the season, he had another five-point game. The Avalanche faced the Minnesota Wild in March 2018. On the power play, MacKinnon held his position at the top of the left circle. He received a pass and then launched a missile that blew past the Wild goalie. MacKinnon finished the night with two goals and three assists, and Colorado stomped Minnesota 7–1.

The Avalanche went back to the playoffs that season for the first time since MacKinnon's rookie year. And MacKinnon had

INTERNATIONAL SUCCESS

Since turning pro and joining the Avalanche, Nathan MacKinnon has also appeared in several international tournaments. In 2015 he had four goals and five assists to help Team Canada win its first World Championship since 2007. And in the 2016 World Cup of Hockey, he scored an amazing backhand goal in overtime to give Team North America a victory over Sweden.

a lot to do with that. He nearly doubled his points total from the year before, finishing with a team-best 97.

The 2018-19 season was MacKinnon's best yet. He led his team to the playoffs for the second year in a row. Colorado faced the mighty Calgary Flames in the first round. In Game 1, Calgary cruised to an easy victory. In Game 2, the score was tied 2-2 at the end of the third period. That meant overtime. In the extra period, Avalanche right winger Mikko Rantanen had the puck along the boards. Meanwhile, MacKinnon streaked down the center of the ice. Rantanen sent him a perfect pass, and MacKinnon took care of the rest. With a wicked wrist shot, he sent the puck screaming into the top corner of the net. The stunned Calgary crowd could only watch as

MacKinnon skates with the puck during a 2019 playoff game against the Calgary Flames.

MacKinnon celebrated his game-winning shot. The Avalanche went on to win the series in five games.

Even though Colorado lost in the next round, Avs fans felt optimistic. With MacKinnon on the team, the future looked bright.

TIMELINE

1. **Springhill, Nova Scotia (September 1, 1995)**
   Nathan MacKinnon is born in Springhill, Nova Scotia.

2. **Halifax, Nova Scotia (December 3, 2011)**
   Playing with the Halifax Mooseheads, MacKinnon scores five goals in one game against the Quebec Remparts.

3. **Saskatoon, Saskatchewan (May 26, 2013)**
   MacKinnon and the Halifax Mooseheads win the Memorial Cup.

4. **Denver, Colorado (October 2, 2013)**
   MacKinnon makes his NHL debut with the Colorado Avalanche. He has two assists in the game.

5. **Washington, DC (October 12, 2013)**
   MacKinnon scores his first NHL goal in a 5-1 win over the Washington Capitals. He also has an assist in the game.

6. **Las Vegas, Nevada (June 24, 2014)**
   At the NHL Awards, MacKinnon becomes the youngest player to receive the Calder Memorial Trophy as the league's rookie of the year.

7. **Los Angeles, California (January 10, 2017)**
   MacKinnon plays in his first NHL All-Star Game.

TO LEARN MORE

Books

Graves, Will. *Ultimate NHL Road Trip*. Minneapolis: Abdo Publishing, 2019.

Peters, Chris. *Hockey Season Ticket: The Ultimate Fan Guide*. Mendota Heights, MN: Press Box Books, 2019.

Peters, Chris. *Hockey's New Wave: The Young Superstars Taking Over the Game*. Mendota Heights, MN: Press Box Books, 2019.

Websites

Career Stats
https://www.hockey-reference.com/players/m/mackina01.html

Colorado Avalanche Official Site
https://www.nhl.com/avalanche

Halifax Mooseheads Official Site
http://halifaxmooseheads.ca/

INDEX

Baie-Comeau Drakkar, 12–13
Benoit, Andre, 18

Calder Memorial Trophy, 21
Calgary Flames, 26
Cole Harbour, Nova Scotia, 11
Crosby, Sidney, 11–12, 15

Girard, Samuel, 24
Gretzky, Wayne, 19

Halifax Mooseheads, 12–14

Landeskog, Gabriel, 6

Minnesota Wild, 20, 25

NHL Entry Draft, 14

Rantanen, Mikko, 26

Shattuck-St. Mary's, 11
St. Louis Blues, 5

Washington Capitals, 24

GLOSSARY

assist
A pass that results in a goal.

debut
First appearance.

draft
An event that allows teams to choose new players coming into the league.

hat trick
A game in which a player scores three or more goals.

point
A statistic that a player earns by scoring a goal or having an assist.

prospect
A player that people expect to do well at a higher level.

rival
An opposing player or team that brings out the greatest emotion from fans and players.

scout
A person who looks for talented young players.

veteran
A player who has spent several years in a league.

AT-A-GLANCE

Birth date: September 1, 1995

Birthplace: Springhill, Nova Scotia

Position: Center

Shoots: Right

Size: 6 feet 0 inches, 205 pounds

NHL team: Colorado Avalanche (2013–)

Previous team: Halifax Mooseheads (2011–2013)

Major awards: NHL All-Star (2017, 2018, 2019), Calder Memorial Trophy (2014), Memorial Cup (2013)

Accurate through the 2018–19 season.

MAP

29